An Explanation of America

Princeton Series of Contemporary Poets
DAVID WAGONER, EDITORIAL ADVISER

Returning Your Call, by Leonard Nathan

Sadness And Happiness, by Robert Pinsky

Burn Down the Icons, by Grace Schulman

Reservations, by James Richardson

The Double Witness: Poems, by Ben Belitt

Night Talk and Other Poems, by Richard Pevear

Listeners at the Breathing Place, by Gary Miranda

The Power to Change Geography, by Diana Ó Hehir

An Explanation of America, by Robert Pinsky

An Explanation of America

ROBERT PINSKY

PRINCETON UNIVERSITY PRESS

PRINCETON, NEW JERSEY

Copyright © 1979 by Princeton University Press
Published by Princeton University Press, 41 William Street,
Princeton, New Jersey 08540
In the United Kingdom: Princeton University Press,
Chichester, West Sussex

Library of Congress Cataloging-in-Publication Data

Pinsky, Robert.
An explanation of America.
(Princeton series of contemporary poets)
I. Title.
PS3566.I54E9   811'.5'4   79-84010
ISBN 0-691-06407-5
ISBN 0-691-01360-8 pbk.

Publication of this book has been aided by a grant from the
Paul Mellon Fund at Princeton University Press

This book has been composed in Linotype Electra

http://pup.princeton.edu

Printed in the United States of America

9 8 7

ACKNOWLEDGMENTS

Poems in this book, and sections of the long poem, first appeared in the following magazines, often in different form and with other titles

"Lair" in *The New Yorker*.

"Memorial" in *The Nation*.

From "An Explanation of America":

Part One, Section I, and Part Three, Section III in *Poetry*.

Part One, Sections II & IV, and Part Two, Section I in *American Poetry Review*; the last of these also appeared in *Agenda* (U.K.).

Part Two, Section III in *New England Review*.

Part Two, Sections III & IV, and Part Three, Section I in *PN Review* (U.K.); the last of these also appeared in *Chicago Review*.

Part Three, Section II in *Canto*.

CONTENTS

LAIR

Inexhaustible, delicate, as if
Without source or medium, daylight
Undoes the mind; the infinite,

Empty actual is too bright,
Scattering to where the road
Whispers, through a mile of woods . . .

Later, how quiet the house is:
Dusk-like and refined,
The sweet Phoebe-note

Piercing from the trees;
The calm globe of the morning,
Things to read or to write

Ranged on a table; the brain
A dark, stubborn current that breathes
Blood, a deaf wadding,

The hands feeding it paper
And sensations of wood or metal
On its own terms. Trying to read

I persist a while, finish the recognition
By my breath of a dead giant's breath—
Stayed by the space of a rhythm,

Witnessing the blue gulf of the air.

1

AN EXPLANATION OF AMERICA

A Poem to my Daughter

Part One:
Its Many Fragments

I. Prologue: You

As though explaining the idea of dancing
Or the idea of some other thing
Which everyone has known a little about
Since they were children, which children learn themselves
With no explaining, but which children like
Sometimes to hear the explanations of,
I want to tell you something about our country,
Or my idea of it: explaining it
If not to you, to my idea of you.

Dancing is the expression by the body
Of how the soul and brain respond to music—
And yes, not only to the sensual, God-like,
Varying repetitions which we love
But also, I admit it, to harmony, too:
As of a group. But what the Brownies did
Gathered inside a church the other day
(Except for one flushed Leader, smiling and skipping
With shoes off through the dance) was Close Drill: frowning,
The children shuffled anxiously at command
Through the home-stitched formations of the Square Dance.
Chewing your nails, you couldn't get it straight.
Another Leader, with her face exalted
By something like a passion after order,
Was roughly steering by the shoulders, each
In turn, two victims: brilliant, incompetent you;
And a tight, humiliated blonde, her daughter.

5

But before going on about groups, leaders,
Churches and such, I think I want to try
To explain you. Countries and people of course
Cannot be known or told in final terms . . .
But can be, in the comic, halting way
Of parents, explained: as Death and Government are.
I don't mean merely to *pretend* to write
To you, yet don't mean either to pretend
To say only what you might want to hear.
I mean to write to my idea of you,
And not expecting you to read a word . . .
Though you are better at understanding words
Than most people I know. You understand
An Old Man's Winter Night. And I believe,
Compulsive explainer that I am, and you
Being who you are, that if I felt the need
To make some smart, professor-ish crack about
Walt Whitman, the Internment Camps, or *Playboy*
I could, if necessary, explain it to you,
Who, writing under the name of "Karen Owens,"
Began your "Essay On Kids": "*In my opinion,
We 'tots' are truly in the 'prime of life,'
Of all creatures on earth, or other planets
Should there be life on such.*"
                              In games and plays,
You like to be the Bad Guy, Clown or Dragon,
Not Mother or The Princess. Your favorite creature

6

Is the Owl, the topic of another "Essay."
Garrulous, prosy, good at spelling and fond
Of punctuation, you cannot form two letters
Alike or on a line. You suck your thumb
And have other infantile traits, although
A student interviewing "tots" from five
To eight for her psychology project found,
Scaling results, that your ideas of God
And of your dreams were those of an adult.
Though I should never tell you that (or this)
It occurs to me, thinking of Chaplin, Twain
And others—thinking of owls, the sacred bird
Of Athens and Athene—that it is not
A type (the solitary flights at night;
The dreams mature, the spirit infantile)
Which America has always known to prize.
—Not that I mean to class you with the great
At your age, but that the celebrated examples
(Ted Williams comes to mind) recall your face,
The soft long lashes behind the owlish glasses
Which you selected over "cuter" frames:
That softness—feathery, protective, inward—
Muffling the quickness of the raptor's eye,
The gaze of liberty and independence
Uneasy in groups and making groups uneasy.

II. *From the Surface*

⌈A country is the things it wants to see.⌉
If so, some part of me, though I do not,
Must want to see these things—as if to say:

"I want to see the calf with two heads suckle;
I want to see the image of a woman
In rapid sequence of transparencies
Projected on a bright flat surface, conveying
The full illusion and effect of motion,
In vast, varying scale, with varying focus,
Swallow the image of her partner's penis.
I want to see enormous colored pictures
Of people with impossible complexions,
Dressed, often, in flamboyant clothes, along
The roads and fastened to the larger buildings.
I want to see men playing games with balls.
I want to see new cars; I want to see
Faces of people, famous, or in times
Of great emotion, or both; and above all,
It seems, I want to see the anthropomorphic
Animals drawn for children, as represented
By people in smiling masks and huge costumes.
I want to shake their hands. I want to see
Cars crashing; cards with a collie or a pipe
And slippers, dry flies, mallards and tennis rackets—
Two people kissing for Valentine, and then
A nicky-nacky design, a little puppy
Begging for me to like the person who mailed it."

In Mexico, I suppose they want to see
The Eyes of God, and dogs and ponies coupling
With women, skeletons in hats and skirts,
Dishwashers, plutocrats humiliated,
Clark Gable, flashy bauhaus buildings, pistols.
It always is disturbing, what a country
Of people want to see. . . . In England once,
A country that I like, between two Terms,
In Oxford, I saw a traveling carnival
And fair with Morris dancers, and a woman
Down in a shallow pit—bored-looking, with bored
And overfed, drugged-looking brown rats lolling
Around her white bare body where it was chained
Among them: sluggish, in a furtive tent.

And that was something, like the Morris dance,
Which an American would neither want
To see, nor think of hiding, which helps to prove
That after all these countries do exist,
All of us sensing what we want to see
Whether we want it separately, or not.

But beyond the kinds of ball or billboard, or what
The woman must undergo, are other proofs,
Suggesting that all countries are the same:
And that the awful, trivial, and atrocious
(Those "forms receptive, featureless and vast")
Are what all peoples want to see and hide,
Are similar everywhere, and every year

9

Take forms that are increasingly the same,
Time and *Der Spiegel*, Chile and Chicago,
All coming to one thing, whether sinister
Or bland as a Christmas card from "Unicef."

What do I want for you to see? I want—
Beyond the states and corporations, each
Hiding and showing after their kind the forms
Of their atrocities, beyond their power
For evil—the greater evil in ourselves,
And greater images more vast than *Time*.
I want for you to see the things I see
And more, Colonial Diners, Disney, films
Of concentration camps, the napalmed child
Trotting through famous newsfilm in her diaper
And tattered flaps of skin, *Deep Throat*, the rest.

I want our country like a common dream
To be between us in what we want to see—
Not that I want for you to have to see
Atrocity itself, or that its image
Is harmless ⌊ I mean the way we need to see
With shared, imperfect memory: the quiet
Of tourists shuffling with their different awes ⌉
Through well-kept Rushmore, Chiswick House, or Belsen;
"Lest we forget" and its half-forgotten aura.
I want for you to see a "hippie restaurant"
And the rock valley where a hundred settlers

10

Were massacred by other settlers, dressed
As Indians—like the Boston tea-tax rioters
Or like the college kids who work for Disney,
Showing the people what they want to see.

III. Local Politics

And so the things the country wants to see
Are like a nest made out of circumstance;
And when, as in the great old sermon "The Eagle
Stirreth Her Nest," God like a nesting eagle
Pulls out a little of the plush around us
And lets the thorns of trial, and the bramble,
Stick through and scrape and threaten the fledgling soul,
We see that that construction of thorn and bramble
Is like a cage: the tight and sheltering cage
Of Law and circumstance, scraping through the plush
Like death—whenever the eagle stirreth her nest,
The body with its bony cage of law
And politics, the thorn of death and taxes.

You, rich in rhetoric and indignation,
The jailbird-lawyer of the Hunnewell School,
Come home from some small, wicked parliament
To elaborate a new theme: forceful topics
Touching the sheeplike, piggish ways of that tyrant
And sycophantic lout, the Majority.
The two lame cheers for democracy that I
Borrow and try to pass to you ("It is
The worst of all the forms of government,
Except for all the others"—Winston Churchill)
You brush aside: Political Science bores you,
You prefer the truth, and with a Jesuit firmness
Return to your slogan: "Voting *is not* fair."

I have another saw that I can scrape
For you, out of the hoard of antique hardware,
Cliches and Great Ideas, quaintly-toothed
Black ironwork that we heap about our young:
Voting is one of the *"necessary evils."*
Avoid all groups and institutions, they
Are necessary evils: necessary
Unto the general Happiness and Safety,
And evil because they are deficient in being.
Such is the hardware; and somewhere in between
The avoidance and the evil necessity
We each conclude a contract with the Beast.

America is, as Malcolm X once said,
A prison. And that the world and all its parts
Are also prisons (Chile, the Hunnewell School,
One's own deficient being, each prison after
Its own degree and kind), does not diminish
Anything that he meant about his country:
When the Dan Ryan Expressway in Chicago
Was flooded, "Black youths" who the paper said
Pillaged the stranded motorists like beached whales
Were rioting prisoners . . . a weight of lead
Sealed in their hearts was lighter for some minutes
Amid the riot.
                    Living inside a prison,
Within its many other prisons, what

Should one aspire to be? a kind of chaplain?
But chaplains, I have heard, are often powers,
Political, within their prisons, patrons
And mediators between the frightened groups:
Blue People, Gray People, and their constricting fears,
The mutual circumstance of ward and warder.

No kind of chaplain ever will mediate
Among the conquering, crazed immigrants
Of El Camino and the Bergen Mall,
The Jews who dream up the cowboy films, the Blacks
Who dream the music, the people who dream the cars
And ways of voting, the Japanese and Basques
Each claiming a special sense of humor, as do
Armenian photo-engravers, and the people
Who dream the saws: *"You cannot let men live
Like pigs, and make them freemen, it is not safe,"*
The people who dream up the new diseases
For use in warfare, the people who design
New shapes of pants, and sandwiches sumptuous
Beyond the dreams of innocent Europe: crazed
As carpet-bombing or the Berlin Airlift—
Crazed immigrants and prisoners, rioting
Or else, alone as in the secrecy
Of a narrow bunk or cell, whittling or painting
Some desperate weapon or crude work of art:
A spoon honed to a dagger or a bauble,
A pistol molded from a cake of soap,
A fumbling poem or a lurid picture

Urgent and sentimental as a tattoo. . . .
The Dorians, too, were conquering immigrants,
And hemmed in by their own anarchic spirits
And new peninsula, they too resorted
To invented institutions, and the vote,
With a spirit nearly comic, and in fear.

The plural-headed Empire, manifold
Beyond my outrage or my admiration,
Is like a prison which I leave to you
(And like a shelter)—where the people vote,
And where the threats of riot and oppression
Inspire the inmates as they whittle, scribble,
Jockey for places in the choir, or smile
Passing out books on weekdays.
                                        On the radio,
The FM station that plays "All Country and Western"
Startled me, when I hit its button one day,
With a voice—inexplicable and earnest—
In Vietnamese or Chinese, lecturing
Or selling, or something someone wanted broadcast,
A paid political announcement, perhaps. . . .
"All politics is local politics"
Said Mayor Daley (in pentameter):
And this then is the locus where we vote,
Prisonyard fulcrum of knowledge, fear and work—
Nest where an Eagle balances and screams,
The wild bird with its hardware in its claws.

15

IV. Countries and Explanations

Gogol explains his country as a troika:
"What Russian doesn't like fast driving," he says,
"Exalted by the dark pines flashing past
Like smoke? . . . And you, my Russia—racing on
To God knows where in an endless, manic blur,
Like the most birdlike troika ever made
By a Russian peasant with an axe and chisel:
No screws, no metal—thundering past the milestones
Like spots before your eyes; and spreading out
Evenly over half the world! . . . A blur;
A jingling of bells, and rattling bridges; the road
Smokes under your wheels as everything falls behind;
The horses take fire, barely touching the earth;
And you become entirely a flow of air,
Inspired by God—Russia, where do you fly?"

She doesn't answer. The air is torn to shreds
And becomes mere wind behind the flying troika;
And the other countries, with nervous glances sideways—
So many pedestrians, startled at the curb—
Step to one side: astonished at the speed
And eloquence of Gogol's explanation,
His country thundering madly down the highway. . . .

Somebody might explain a troubled time
By saying, "It's because they killed the railroads":
Because a child who hears a whistle at night
Can hear it drawing closer to the bed
And further in a line, along a vein,

While highways murmuring in the night are like
A restless river, grown unpredictable
A way that rivers don't.
                              And yet the shadows
From headlights as they circled my bedroom walls
Have given me comfort too, the lights and whistle
Like two different sentimental songs
At night. And though the cars and highways do stifle
The downtowns and their sweet co-operation
(The City Bakery, the Paramount, the stores)
I love a car—a car, I guess, is like
One's personality, corrupt and selfish,
Full of hypnotic petty pains and joys,
While riding on a train is like the mind,
The separate reveries, the communal rhythm
Of motion in a line, along a vein. . . .

The communal speed of trains and happy freedom
In a car are like the troika: speed making plain
The great size of its place, the exhilaration
Of change which the size evokes—the schedules, pillows
And porters on the train, the thrill of wit
And aggression in a car, choosing a lane—
Yet some day, tamed and seasoned, our machines
Might make plain that America is a country:
Another country like others with their myths
Of their uniqueness, Tara and Golden Peru
And headlong Mother Russia or Colombia,
Finlandia and the Cowboy's Prayer, and even

Quiet Helvetia; each place a country
With myths and anthems and its heroic name.

And motion would be a place, and who knows, you
May live there in the famous national "love
Of speed" as though in some small town where children
Walk past their surnames in the churchyard, you
At home among the murmur of that place
Unthinkable for me, but for the children
Of that place comforting as an iceman's horse.

⎰ Because as all things have their explanations,
⎱ True or false, all can come to seem domestic. ⎤
The brick mills of New England on their rivers
Are *brooding, classic*; the Iron Horse is quaint,
Steel oildrums, musical; and the ugly suburban
"Villas" of London, Victorian Levittowns,
Have come to be civilized and urbane.

And so, although a famous wanderer
Defines a nation, "The same people living
In the same place," by such strange transformations
Of time the motion from place to place itself
May come to be the place we have in common.
The regions and their ways—like Northern Michigan
And its Rutabaga Pasties, or Union City
With its Cuban and Armenian churches—will be
As though Officially Protected Species.
The Shopping Center itself will be as precious

And quaint as is the threadmill now converted
Into a quaint and high-class shopping center.
For *place*, itself, is always a kind of motion,
A part of it artificial and preserved,
And a part born in a blur of loss and change—
All places in motion from where we thought they were,
Boston before it was Irish or Italian,
Harlem and Long Branch before we ever knew
That they were beautiful, and when they were:
Our nation, mellowing to another country
Of different people living in different places.

Part Two:
Its Great Emptiness

I. A Love of Death

Imagine a child from Virginia or New Hampshire
Alone on the prairie eighty years ago
Or more, one afternoon—the shaggy pelt
Of grasses, for the first time in that child's life,
Flowing for miles. Imagine the moving shadow
Of a cloud far off across that shadeless ocean,
The obliterating strangeness like a tide
That pulls or empties the bubble of the child's
Imaginary heart. No hills, no trees.

The child's heart lightens, tending like a bubble
Towards the currents of the grass and sky,
The pure potential of the clear blank spaces.

Or, imagine the child in a draw that holds a garden
Cupped from the limitless motion of the prairie,
Head resting against a pumpkin, in evening sun.
Ground-cherry bushes grow along the furrows,
The fruit red under its papery, moth-shaped sheath.
Grasshoppers tumble among the vines, as large
As dragons in the crumbs of pale dry earth.
The ground is warm to the child's cheek, and the wind
Is a humming sound in the grass above the draw,
Rippling the shadows of the red-green blades.
The bubble of the child's heart melts a little,

21

Because the quiet of that air and earth
Is like the shadow of a peaceful death—
Limitless and potential, a kind of space
Where one dissolves to become a part of something
Entire . . . whether of sun and air, or goodness
And knowledge, it does not matter to the child.

Dissolved among the particles of the garden
Or into the motion of the grass and air,
Imagine the child happy to be a thing.

Imagine, then, that on that same wide prairie
Some people are threshing in the terrible heat
With horses and machines, cutting bands
And shoveling amid the clatter of the threshers,
The chaff in prickly clouds and the naked sun
Burning as if it could set the chaff on fire.
Imagine that the people are Swedes or Germans,
Some of them resting pressed against the strawstacks,
Trying to get the meager shade.
                                        A man,
A tramp, comes laboring across the stubble
Like a mirage against that blank horizon,
Laboring in his torn shoes toward the tall
Mirage-like images of the tilted threshers
Clattering in the heat. Because the Swedes
Or Germans have no beer, or else because
They cannot speak his language properly,
Or for some reason one cannot imagine,

The man climbs up on a thresher and cuts bands
A minute or two, then waves to one of the people,
A young girl or a child, and jumps head-first
Into the sucking mouth of the machine,
Where he is wedged and beat and cut to pieces—
While the people shout and run in the clouds of chaff,
Like lost mirages on the pelt of prairie.

The obliterating strangeness and the spaces
Are as hard to imagine as the love of death . . .
Which is the love of an entire strangeness,
The contagious blankness of a quiet plain.
Imagine that a man, who had seen a prairie,
Should write a poem about a Dark or Shadow
That seemed to be both his, and the prairie's—as if
The shadow proved that he was not a man,
But something that lived in quiet, like the grass.
Imagine that the man who writes that poem,
Stunned by the loneliness of that wide pelt,
Should prove to himself that he was like a shadow
Or like an animal living in the dark.

In the dark proof he finds in his poem, the man
Might come to think of himself as the very prairie,
The sod itself, not lonely, and immune to death.

None of this happens precisely as I try
To imagine that it does, in the empty plains,
And yet it happens in the imagination

Of part of the country: not in any place
More than another, on the map, but rather
Like a place, where you and I have never been
And need to try to imagine—place like a prairie
Where immigrants, in the obliterating strangeness,
Thirst for the wide contagion of the shadow
Or prairie—where you and I, with our other ways,
More like the cities or the hills or trees,
Less like the clear blank spaces with their potential,
Are like strangers in a place we must imagine.

II. Bad Dreams

In a way, every stranger must imagine
The place where he finds himself—as shrewd Odysseus
Was able to imagine, as he wandered,
The ways and perils of a foreign place:
Making his goal, not knowing the real place,
But his survival, and his progress home.
And everyone has felt it—foreign ground,
With its demand on the imagination
Like the strange gaze of the cattle of the Sun—
Unless one is an angel, or a hick,
A tribesman who never made his wander-year.

People who must, like immigrants or nomads,
Live always in imaginary places
Think of some past or word to fill a blank—
The encampment at the Pole or at the Summit;
Comanches in Los Angeles; the Jews
Of Russia or Roumania, who lived
In Israel before it was a place or thought,
But a pure, memorized word which they knew better
Than their own hands.
                        And at the best such people,
However desperate, have a lightness of heart
That comes to the mind alert among its reasons,
A sense of the arbitrariness of the senses:
Blank snow subordinate to the textbook North.
Like tribesmen living in a real place,
With their games, jokes or gossip, a love of skill
And commerce, they keep from loving the blank of death.

But there are perils in living always in vision—
Always inventing entire whatever paves
Or animates the innocent sand or snow
Of a mere locale. What if the place itself
Should seem a blank, as in a country huge
And open and potential? . . . the blank enlarges,
And swelling in concentric gusts of quiet
Absorbs the imagination in a cloud
Of quiet, as smoke disperses through a mist,
A vague chimera that engulfs the breath.

That quiet leads me to a stranger's dread
Of the place frightened settlers might invent:
The customs of the people there, the tongues
They speak, and what they have to drink, the things
That they imagine, might falter in such a place,
Or be too few; and men would live like Cyclopes,
"With neither assemblies nor any settled customs"—
Or Laestrygonians who consume their kind
And see a stranger as his meat and marrow,
And have no cities or cultivated farms.

A man who eats the lotus of his prairie
Or shadow—consumed by his desire for darkness
Till the mind seems itself a dreamy marrow—
Is like those creatures of a traveler's nightmare.
Even his sentiments about the deer,
Or grass, recall man-eating Polyphemus:
Who, when he cracks like a movie Nazi, sheds

Real tears, making a sentimental speech
To his pet ram.
                    In place of settled customs,
Such a man might set up a brazen calf,
Or join a movement, fanatical, to spite
The spirit of assembly, or of words—
To drown that chatter and gossip, and become
Sure, like machines and animals and the earth.

Such a man—neither a Greek adventurer
With his pragmatic gods, nor an Indian,
Nor Jew—would worship, not an earth or past
Or word, but something immanent, like a shadow . . .
Perhaps he was once a Protestant, with a God
Whose hand was in every berry, insect, cloud:
Not in the Indian way, but as one hand,
Immanent, above that berry and its name.

And when that hand came to him as a prairie
He beheld pure space as if it were a god,
Or as a devil. And if he lost that hand,
Why wouldn't he—in his loneliness and love
Of thinking nothing—grow eager to lose himself
Among a brazen crowd, as in a calf,
A certain landscape, or a bird?
                              Or say
That he sets out upon that empty plain
Immanent with a quiet beyond all thought
Or words, and that he settles on that ground

Of trial, to invent a mystic home—
And then discovers people there, engaged
Upon their commerce or their gossip, at home
Or wandering as in an actual place,
Attending to their ordinary business:
The ordinary passion to bring death
For gain or glory, as Odysseus
Might feel, would be augmented and inflamed
By the harsh passion of a settler; and so,
Why wouldn't he bring his death to Indians
Or Jews, or Greeks who stop for food and water,
To bustle and jabber on his tangled plain?

But my nightmare is not the one you have
To fear, exactly, and if the Cyclops comes
(Lumbering, hungry, unreasoning, drunk or blind)
He may come gently, without commotion, cloaked
More in the manner—as in poems by Auden—
Of a disquieting nurse, an official form
With its inquiry, than of my bad dreams.

For I am father and mother of my man
(Who is no man, but something I imagined,
Or a kind of word for something that I fear),
And perhaps I am his child, too: choosing to be
Myself explaining him, or him—like people
Who have mixed blood, and might feel free to choose
To be themselves as Indians, or Cowboys . . .
With their high cheekbones, blue eyes, and iron hair.

And you and I, who have no Indian blood
(Or Cowboy blood, assuming such a thing)
Imagine two sides of people—with their blood,
A place, a climate, their circumstances fixed
As bounds for choice or for imagination—
Hardly free: the takers ready to kill
To take the theater of their imagined home,
Still half imaginary; the defenders
At home in places that became the more
Imaginary as the white ones took
Tobacco; taught scalping; introduced the horse.

And even Malcolm X, who changed his name
So many times, whom we remember now
Most by that one name which still means "unknown"—
Possibly "free"—must, with his many names
And his red hair, have needed to consider
The kinds of arbitrariness and choice:
The arbitrariness of the blood and senses
Compared to the poles and summits of our choosing,
The textbook "Indian," "American" or "blood" . . .
The accumulating prison of the past
That pulls us towards a body and a place.

My imaginary man is in that prison,
Though he thinks only of the feral earth,
Making himself less free.
                              Then let him rest;
And think instead of the European poets

Posed thoughtfully with cigarettes or scarves,
As photographed for a fascist anthology
Of forty years ago, above their verses
About a landscape, tribe, or mystic shadow:
Caught in the prison of their country's earth
Or its Romantic potential, born of death
Or of a pure idea. ". . . *Italy*
(Germany, Russia, America, Roumania)
Had never really been a country," a book
Might say, explaining something.

                                        What I want

And want for you is not a mystic home
But something—if it must be imaginary—
Chosen from life, and useful. Nietzsche says
We should admire the traffickers and nomads

"Who have that freedom of the mind and soul
Which mankind learns from frequent changes of place,
Climate and customs, new neighbors and oppressors."

Americans, we choose to see ourselves
As here, yet not here yet—as if a Roman
In mid-Rome should inquire the way to Rome.
Like Jews or Indians, roving on the plains
Of places taken from us, or imagined,
We accumulate the customs, music, words
Of different climates, neighbors and oppressors,
Making encampment in the sand or snow.

Sense of place imagined? Is this engrained in our culture & ideals?

30

III. Horace, Epistulæ *I, xvi*

The poet Horace, writing to a friend
About his Sabine farm and other matters,
Implies his answer about aspiration
Within the prison of empire or republic:

"Dear Quinctius:
                I'll tell you a little about
My farm—in case you ever happen to wonder
About the place: as, what I make in grain,
Or if I'm getting rich on olives, apples,
Timber or pasture.
                There are hills, unbroken
Except for one soft valley, cut at an angle
That sweetens the climate, because it takes the sun
All morning on its right slope, until the left
Has its turn, warming as the sun drives past
All afternoon. You'd like it here: the plums
And low-bush berries are ripe; and where my cows
Fill up on acorns and ilex-berries a lush
Canopy of shade gives pleasure to their master.
The green is deep, so deep you'd say Tarentum
Had somehow nestled closer, to be near Rome.

There is a spring, fit for a famous river
(The Hebrus winds through Thrace no colder or purer),
Useful for healing stomach-aches and head-aches.
And here I keep myself, and the place keeps me—
A precious good, believe it, Quinctius—
In health and sweetness through September's heat.

31

You of course live in the way that is truly right,
If you've been careful to remain the man
That we all see in you. We here in Rome
Talk of you, always, as 'happy' . . . there is the fear,
Of course, that one might listen too much to others,
Think what they see, and strive to be that thing,
And lose by slow degrees that inward man
Others first noticed—as though, if over and over
Everyone tells you you're in marvelous health,
You might towards dinner-time, when a latent fever
Falls on you, try for a long while to disguise it,
Until the trembling rattles your food-smeared hands.
It's foolishness to camouflage our sores.

Take 'recognition'—what if someone writes
A speech about your service to your country,
Telling for your attentive ears the roll
Of all your victories by land or sea,
With choice quotations, dignified periods,
And skillful terms, all in the second person,
As in the citations for honorary degrees:
'Only a mind beyond our human powers
Could judge if your great love for Rome exceeds,
Or is exceeded by, Rome's need for you.'

—You'd find it thrilling, but inappropriate
For anyone alive, except Augustus.

And yet if someone calls me 'wise' or 'flawless'

Must one protest? I like to be told I'm right,
And brilliant, as much as any other man.
The trouble is, the people who give out
The recognition, compliments, degrees
Can take them back tomorrow, if they choose;
The committee or electorate decide
You can't sit in the Senate, or have the Prize—
'Sorry, but isn't that ours, that you nearly took?'
What can I do, but shuffle sadly off?
If the same people scream that I'm a crook
Who'd strangle my father for money to buy a drink,
Should I turn white with pain and humiliation?
If prizes and insults from outside have much power
To hurt or give joy, something is sick inside.

Who is 'the good man'?
                    Many people would answer,
'He is the man who never breaks the law
Or violates our codes. His judgment is sound.
He is the man whose word is as his bond.
If such a man agrees to be your witness,
Your case is won.'
                    And yet this very man,
If you ask his family, or the people who know him,
Is like a rotten egg in its flawless shell.
And if a slave or prisoner should say
'I never steal; I never try to escape,'
My answer is, 'You have your just rewards:
No beatings; no solitary; and your food.'

'I have not killed.' 'You won't be crucified.'
'But haven't I shown that I am good, and honest?'

To this, my country neighbor would shake his head
And sigh: 'Ah no! The wolf himself is wary
Because he fears the pit, as hawks the snare
Or pike the hook. Some folk hate vice for love
Of the good: you're merely afraid of guards and crosses.'

Apply that peasant wisdom to that 'good man'
Of forum and tribunal, who in the temple
Calls loudly on 'Father Janus' or 'Apollo'
But in an undertone implores, 'Laverna,
Goddess of thieves, O Fair One, grant me, please,
That I get away with it, let me pass as upright,
Cover my sins with darkness, my lies with clouds.'

When a man stoops to pluck at the coin some boys
Of Rome have soldered to the street, I think
That just then he is no more free than any
Prisoner, or slave; it seems that someone who wants
Too much to get things is also someone who fears,
And living in that fear cannot be free.
A man has thrown away his weapons, has quit
The struggle for virtue, who is always busy
Filling his wants, getting things, making hay—
Weaponless and defenseless as a captive.

When you have got a captive, you never kill him

If you can sell him for a slave; this man
Truly will make a good slave: persevering,
Ambitious, eager to please—as ploughman, or shepherd,
Or trader plying your goods at sea all winter,
Or helping to carry fodder at the farm. . . .
The truly good, and wise man has more courage;
And if need be, will find the freedom to say,
As in the *Bacchae* of Euripides:

King Pentheus, Lord of Thebes, what will you force me
To suffer at your hands?
                              I will take your goods.

You mean my cattle, furniture, cloth and plate?
Then you may have them.
                              I will put you, chained,
Into my prison, under a cruel guard.

Then God himself, the moment that I choose,
Will set me free. . . .

I think that what this means is: 'I will die.'

Death is the chalk-line towards which all things race."

IV. Filling the Blank

Odd, that the poet who seems so complacent
About his acorns and his cold pure water,
Writing from his retreat just out of Rome,
Should seem to end with a different love of death
From that of someone on a mystic plain—
But still, with love of death. ". . . A rather short man,"
He calls himself, "and prematurely gray,
Who liked to sit in the sun; a freedman's child
Who spread his wings too wide for that frail nest
And yet found favor, in both war and peace,
With powerful men. Tell them I lost my temper
Easily, but was easily appeased,
My book—and if they chance to ask my age
Say, I completed my forty-fourth December
In the first year that Lepidus was Consul."

I think that what the poet meant was this:
That freedom, even in a free Republic,
Rests ultimately on the right to die.
And though he's careful to say that Quinctius,
The public man able to act for good
And help his fellow-Romans, lives the life
That truly is the best, he's also careful
To separate their fortunes and their places,
And to appreciate his own: his health,
His cows and acorns and his healing spring,
His circle—"*We here in Rome*"—for friends and gossip.

It would be too complacent to build a nest

Between one's fatalism and one's pleasures—
With death at one side, a sweet farm at the other,
Keeping the thorns of government away. . . .

Horace's father, who had been a slave,
Engaged in some small business near Venusia;
And like a Jewish or Armenian merchant
Who does well in America, he sent
His son to Rome's best schools, and then to Athens
(It's hard to keep from thinking "as to Harvard")
To study, with the sons of gentlemen
And politicians, the higher arts most useful
To citizens of a Republic: math;
Philosophy; rhetoric in all its branches.

One March, when Horace, not quite twenty-one,
Was still at Athens, Julius Caesar died,
And the Roman world was split by civil war.

When Brutus came to Athens late that summer
On his way to Asia Minor—"half-mystical,
Wholly romantic Brutus"—Horace quit school
To follow Brutus to Asia, bearing the title
Or brevet-commission *tribunus militum*,
And served on the staff of the patriot-assassin.

Time passed; the father died; the property
And business were lost, or confiscated.
The son saw action at Philippi, where,

Along with other enthusiastic students
(Cicero's son among them), and tens of thousands
In the two largest armies of Roman soldiers
Ever to fight with one another, he shared
In the republican army's final rout
By Antony and Octavian.
                              Plutarch says
That Brutus, just before he killed himself,
Speaking in Greek to an old fellow-student,
Said that although he was angry for his country
He was deeply happy for himself—because
His virtue and his repute for virtue were founded
In a way none of the conquerors could hope,
For all their arms and riches, to emulate;
Nor could they hinder posterity from knowing,
And saying, that they were unjust and wicked men
Who had destroyed justice and the Republic,
Usurping a power to which they had no right.

The corpse of Brutus was found by Antony,
And he commanded the richest purple mantle
In his possession to be thrown over it,
And afterwards, the mantle being stolen,
He found the thief and had him put to death;
The ashes of Brutus he sent back to Rome,
To be received with honor by the mourners.

Horace came back to Rome a pardoned rebel
In his late twenties, without cash or prospects,

Having stretched out his wings too far beyond
The frail nest of his freedman father's hopes,
As he has written.
                    When he was thirty-five,
He published some poems which some people praised,
And so through Vergil he met the Roman knight
And good friend of Augustus, called Maecenas,
Who befriended him, and gave him the Sabine farm;
And in that place, and in the highest circles
In Rome itself, he spent his time, and wrote.

Since aspirations need not (some say, should not)
Be likely, should I wish for you to be
A hero, like Brutus—who at the finish-line
Declared himself to be a happy man?
Or is the right wish health, the just proportion
Of sun, the acorns and cold pure water, a nest
Out in the country and a place in Rome . . .

Of course, one's aspirations must depend
Upon the opportunities: the justice
That happens to be available; one's fortune.
I think that what the poet meant may be
Something like that; and as for aspiration,
Maybe our aspirations for ourselves
Ought to be different from the hopes we have
(Though there are warnings against too much hope)
When thinking of our children. And in fact
Our fantasies about the perfect life

Are different for ourselves and for our children,
Theirs being safer, less exciting, purer—
And so, depending always on the chances
Our country offers, it seems we should aspire,
For ourselves, to struggle actively to save
The Republic—or to be, if not like Brutus,
Like Quinctius: a citizen of affairs,
Free in the state and in the love of death . . .
While for our children we are bound to aspire
Differently: something like a nest or farm;
So that the cycle of different aspirations
Threads through posterity.
                              And who can say
What Brutus may come sweeping through your twenties—
Given the taste you have for noble speeches,
For causes lost and glamourous and just.

Did Horace's father, with his middle-class
And slavish aspirations, have it right?—
To give your child the education fit
For the upper classes: math, philosophy,
And rhetoric in all its branches; so I
Must want for you, when you must fall upon
The sword of government or mortality—
Since all of us, even you, race toward it—to have
The power to make your parting speech in Greek
(Or in the best equivalent) and if
You ever write for fame or money, that Vergil
Will pick your book out from a hundred others,
If that's not plucking at a soldered coin.

Part Three:
Its Everlasting Possibility

I. Braveries

Once, while a famous town lay torn and burning
A woman came to childbed, and lay in labor
While all around her people cursed and screamed
In desperation, and soldiers raged insanely—
So that the child came out, the story says,
In the loud center of every horror of war.
And looking on that scene, just halfway out,
The child retreated backward, to the womb:
And chose to make those quiet walls its urn.

"*Brave infant of Saguntum*," a poet says—
As though to embrace a limit might show courage.
(Although the word is more like *bravo*, the glory
Of a great tenor, the swagger of new clothes:
The infant as a brilliant moral performer
Defying in its retreat the bounds of life.)

Denial of limit has been the pride, or failing,
Well-known to be shared by all this country's regions,
Races, and classes; which all seem to challenge
The idea of sufficiency itself . . .
And while it seems that in the name of limit
Some people are choosing to have fewer children,
Or none, that too can be a gesture of freedom—
A way to deny or brave the bounds of time.

41

A boundary is a limit. How can I
Describe for you the boundaries of this place
Where we were born: where Possibility spreads
And multiplies and exhausts itself in growing,
And opens yawning to swallow itself again?
What pictures are there for that limitless grace
Unrealized, those horizons ever dissolving?

A field house built of corrugated metal,
The frosted windows tilted open inward
In two lines high along the metal walls;
Inside, a horse-ring and a horse called Yankee
Jogging around the ring with clouds of dust
Rising and settling in the still, cold air
Behind the horse and rider as they course
Rhythmically through the bars of washed-out light
That fall in dim arcades all down the building.

The rider, a girl of seven or eight called Rose,
Concentrates firmly on her art, her body,
Her small, straight back and shoulders as they rise
Together with the alternate, gray shoulders
Of the unweary horse. Her father stands
And watches, in a business suit and coat,
Watching the child's face under the black serge helmet,
Her yellow hair that bounces at her nape
And part-way down her back. He feels the cold
Of the dry, sunless earth up through the soles
Of his thin, inappropriate dress shoes.

He feels the limit of that simple cold,
And braves it, concentrating on the progress
Of the child riding in circles around the ring.
She is so charming that he feels less mortal.
As from the bravery of a fancy suit,
He takes crude courage from the ancient meaning
Of the horse, as from a big car or a business:
He feels as if the world had fewer limits.
The primitive symbols of the horse and girl
Seem goods profound and infinite, as clear
As why the stuffs of merchants are called, "goods."

The goods of all the world seem possible
And clear in that brave spectacle, the rise
Up from the earth and onto the property
Of horses and the history of riding.

In his vague yearning, as he muses on goods
Lost and confused as chivalry, he might
Dream anything: as from the Cavalier
One might dream up the Rodeo, or the Ford,
Or some new thing the country waited for—
Some property, some consuming peasant dream
Of horses and walls; as though the Rodeo
And Ford were elegiac gestures; as though
Invented things gave birth to long-lost goods.

The country, boasting that it cannot see
The past, waits dreaming ever of the past,

Or all the plural pasts: the way a fetus
Dreams vaguely of heaven—waiting, and in its courage
Willing, not only to be born out into
The Actual (with its ambiguous goods),
But to retreat again and be born backward
Into the gallant walls of its potential,
Its sheltered circle . . . willing to leave behind,
It might be, carnage.
                    What shall we keep open—
Where shall we throw our courage, where retreat?

White settlers disembarked here, to embark
Upon a mountain-top of huge potential—
Which for the disembarking slaves was low:
A swamp, or valley of dry bones, where they lay
In labor with a brilliant, strange slave-culture—
All emigrants, ever disembarking. *Shall these
Bones live?* And in a jangle of confusion
And hunger, from the mountains to the valleys,
They rise; and breathe; and fall in the wind again.

II. Serpent Knowledge

In something you have written in school, you say
That snakes are born (or hatched) already knowing
Everything they will ever need to know—
Weazened and prematurely shrewd, like Merlin;
Something you read somewhere, I think, some textbook
Coy on the subject of the reptile brain.
(Perhaps the author half-remembered reading
About the Serpent of Experience
That changes manna to gall.) I don't believe it;
Even a snake's horizon must expand,
Inwardly, when an instinct is confirmed
By some new stage of life: to mate, kill, die.

Like angels, who have no genitals or place
Of national origin, however, snakes
Are not historical creatures; unlike chickens,
Who teach their chicks to scratch the dust for food—
Or people, who teach ours how to spell their names:
Not born already knowing all we need,
One generation differing from the next
In what it needs, and knows.
                              So what I know,
What you know, what your sister knows (approaching
The age you were when I began this poem)
All differ, like different overlapping stretches
Of the same highway: with different lacks, and visions.
The words—"*Vietnam*"—that I can't use in poems
Without the one word threatening to gape
And swallow and enclose the poem, for you
May grow more finite; able to be touched.

The actual highway—snake's-back where it seems
That any strange thing may be happening, now,
Somewhere along its endless length—once twisted
And straightened, and took us past a vivid place:
Brave in the isolation of its profile,
"Ten miles from nowhere" on the rolling range,
A family graveyard on an Indian mound
Or little elevation above the grassland. . . .
Fenced in against the sky's huge vault at dusk
By a waist-high iron fence with spear-head tips,
The grass around and over the mound like surf.

A mile more down the flat fast road, the homestead:
Regretted, vertical, and unadorned
As its white gravestones on their lonely mound—
Abandoned now, the paneless windows breathing
Easily in the wind, and no more need
For courage to survive the open range
With just the graveyard for a nearest neighbor;
The stones of Limit—comforting and depriving.

Elsewhere along the highway, other limits—
Hanging in shades of neon from dusk to dusk,
The signs of people who know how to take
Pleasure in places where it seems unlikely:
New kinds of places, the "overdeveloped" strips
With their arousing, vacant-minded jumble;
Or garbagey lake-towns, and the tourist-pits
Where crimes unspeakably bizarre come true

To astonish countries older, or more savage . . .
As though the rapes and murders of the French
Or Indonesians were less inventive than ours,
Less goofy than those happenings that grow
Like air-plants—out of nothing, and alone.

They make us parents want to keep our children
Locked up, safe even from the daily papers
That keep the grisly record of that frontier
Where things unspeakable happen along the highways.

In today's paper,'you see the teen-aged girl
From down the street; camping in Oregon
At the far point of a trip across the country,
Together with another girl her age,
They suffered and survived a random evil.
An unidentified, youngish man in jeans
Aimed his car off the highway, into the park
And at their tent (apparently at random)
And drove it over them once, and then again;
And then got out, and struck at them with a hatchet
Over and over, while they struggled; until
From fear, or for some other reason, or none,
He stopped; and got back into his car again
And drove off down the night-time highway. No rape,
No robbery, no "motive." Not even words,
Or any sound from him that they remember.
The girl still conscious, by crawling, reached the road

And even some way down it; where some people
Drove by and saw her, and brought them both to help,
So doctors could save them—barely marked.
                                                    You see
Our neighbor's picture in the paper: smiling,
A pretty child with a kerchief on her head
Covering where the surgeons had to shave it.
You read the story, and in a peculiar tone—
Factual, not unfeeling, like two policemen—
Discuss it with your sister. You seem to feel
Comforted that it happened far away,
As in a crazy place, in *Oregon*:
For me, a place of wholesome reputation;
For you, a highway where strangers go amok,
As in the universal provincial myth
That sees, in every stranger, a mad attacker . . .
(And in one's victims, it may be, a stranger).

Strangers: the Foreign who, coupling with their cousins
Or with their livestock, or even with wild beasts,
Spawn children with tails, or claws and spotted fur,
Ugly—and though their daughters are beautiful
Seen dancing from the front, behind their backs
Or underneath their garments are the tails
Of reptiles, or teeth of bears.
                                        So one might feel—
Thinking about the people who cross the mountains
And oceans of the earth with separate legends,
To die inside the squalor of sod huts,

48

Shanties, or tenements; and leave behind
Their legends, or the legend of themselves,
Broken and mended by the generations:
Their alien, orphaned, and disconsolate spooks,
Earth-trolls or Kallikaks or Snopes or golems,
Descended of Hessians, runaway slaves and Indians,
Legends confused and loose on the roads at night . . .
The Alien or Creature of the movies.

As people die, their monsters grow more tame;
So that the people who survived Saguntum,
Or in the towns that saw the Thirty Years' War,
Must have felt that the wash of blood and horror
Changed something, inside. Perhaps they came to see
The state or empire as a kind of Whale
Or Serpent, in whose body they must live—
Not that mere suffering could make us wiser,
Or nobler, but only older, and more ourselves. . . .

On television, I used to see, each week,
Americans descending in machines
With wasted bravery and blood; to spread
Pain and vast fires amid a foreign place,
Among the strangers to whom we were new—
Americans: a spook or golem, there.
I think it made our country older, forever.
I don't mean better or not better, but merely
As though a person should come to a certain place
And have his hair turn gray, that very night.

Someday, the War in Southeast Asia, somewhere—
Perhaps for you and people younger than you—
Will be the kind of history and pain
Saguntum is for me; but never tamed
Or "history" for me, I think. I think
That I may always feel as if I lived
In a time when the country aged itself:
[More lonely together in our common strangeness . . .]
As if we were a family, and some members
Had done an awful thing on a road at night,
And all of us had grown white hair, or tails:
And though the tails or white hair would afflict
Only that generation then alive
And of a certain age, regardless whether
They were the ones that did or planned the thing—
Or even heard about it—nevertheless
The members of that family ever after
Would bear some consequence or demarcation,
Forgotten maybe, taken for granted, a trait,
A new syllable buried in their name.

III. Mysteries of the Future

People stream slowly from a city church,
Their clothes bright in the sudden winter daylight,
Their bodies clean and warm inside the cloth
Like flags and armor in the dazzling air,
Sun flashing and wincing from the curbside ice.
Their pace is dreamy, strolling to their cars
Over the gritty sidewalk, in Sunday clothes.

It is Chicago; and though in many ways
It could be some place in another country,
The way I see the people and the church—
As mysteries, not just unknown or foreign—
Makes it this country: and Chicago, a setting
We make as we discover. It makes me think
Of how small children, with laborious
And grubby fingers, improvise a scene
From disproportionate, inspired arrangements
Of toys and objects: mirror for a pond,
And gathered on the shore amid strange buildings,
In mad, pedantic order, animals
And people. The squirrel, immense, bears on his shoulders
Riders including an anthropomorphic lion,
In pants and glasses. Barnyard and jungle creatures
Have landed their airplane—some are on the wings—
Right on the hotel roof. Wagons and cars
Parade down to the water. . . .
                                    The girls and women
In pretty colors, the males in blue or brown,
Pause eddying on the steps, as though to blink
Like science-fiction travelers through time,

Uncertain if the surfaces they see
So brazenly gleaming mean to hail them toward
The mysteries of the past, or of the future.

Whether they have slept in church or not, they look
Refreshed in spirit, ready for the cuisine
And music of this era ahead or back,
Younger or older than the one they knew.

"For here we have no continuing city, but seek
For one to come"—*Hebrews*, 13 : 14.
I can't say if our country is old, or young.
The future is an electrocuting thought—
That stuns the thinking reed to quiet, and heightens
The sense that everything we make is mortal,
Or part of some continuing epitaph.
Our very sentences are like a cloth
Cut shimmering from conventions of the dead—
Hung sometimes to flutter from a spar or gallant,
Nudged forward like the paper boats of candy
Launched for the gods downriver, in the future.

If I could sail forward to see the streets
Of that strange country where you will live past me,
Or further even by a hundred years;
And walk those pavements with my phantom steps,
And find Chicago flashing in winter sun;
And church doors ready to swing open, or melt
Before my penetrating ghost—my courage

Would fail, I think: best not to mount the steps
Where I could leave no footprint in the snow . . .
Best not to see those garments.
                              The shining casket,
Pure gold, where Philip of Macedonia lay
Twenty-three hundred years, and his breastplate
And greaves of gold and ivory, are gorgeous still;
But all the treasury of woven fabrics
And splendid leather that lay around the king
Technicians using instruments can deduce
Only from the fine dust scattered on the floor
Around the casket; the long hardwood handle
Of his bright spear fell slowly to a powder
Where it was propped, and left the point adhering
Eerily to the stonework of the wall.

It's fearful to leave anything behind,
To choose or make some one thing to survive
Into the future—where the air and light
That spread around us here in all directions
Stand ready to dim, discolor, and unravel
The colors that we fit around our bodies,
Precious and mutable, a second skin.
(Although the soul may be immortal, or not—
And some believe that even the body may rise—
Our cloth must die, and parch away forever.)

Jefferson in his epitaph records
That he was author of the Declaration

Of Independence, and of the Virginia law
Providing public education; and founder
Of that state's University—omitting
His "high office" . . . as if it were a bound,
Or something held, not something he had done—
The ceremonial garment he had been given
By others, with a certain solemn function
And honor; eventually, to be removed.

The church, Gothic Revival, and waiting cars
With brightwork glinting through a haze of salt
Suggest Nostalgia and Progress—which are in spirit
Less blatant, intimate, tragic than Epitaph:
As though the people, blood rising to their cheeks
As they walk into the cold, could leave behind
The image of themselves in their good clothes—
To survive as a memorial, compacted
By twenty centuries of the slowest fire
As if to something made of stone, or metal.

In the familiar boast or accusation
Americans have scant "historic sense";
Nostalgia and Progress seem to be our frail
National gestures against the enveloping,
Suffusive nightmare of time—which swallows first
The unaware, because they are least free . . .
But time's nightmare, and freedom from it, differ
For different peoples: like their burial customs;
And what they choose to say in what they leave.

To speak words few enough to fit a stone,
And frame them as if speaking from the past
Into the void or mystery of the future,
Demands that we be naked, free, and final:

> *God wills us free, man wills us slaves.*
> *I will as God wills Gods will be done.*
> *Here lies the body of*
> **JOHN JACK**
> *A native of Africa who died*
> *MARCH 1773 aged about 60 years*
>
> *Tho' born in a land of slavery,*
> *He was born free,*
> *Tho' he lived in a land of liberty,*
> *He lived a slave,*
> *Till by his honest, tho' stolen labors,*
> *He acquired the source of slavery,*
> *Which gave him his freedom,*
> *Tho' not long before*
> *Death the Grand Tyrant*
> *Gave him his final emancipation,*
> *And set him on a footing with kings.*
> *Tho' a slave to vice,*
> *He practiced those virtues*
> *Without which kings are but slaves.*

IV. *Epilogue*: *Endings*

"Pregnant again with the old twins, Hope and Fear" . . .
I'll write you one more time. You're older now,
By three years. And when the college students do
The Winter's Tale, you're charming as Mammilius,
The small bold Prince who starts what seems to be
A story about a ghost, and dies offstage
Before Act III is over—in time for bedtime,
Though you prefer to stay through each rehearsal,
As pleased as Puck, among the all-girl cast:
A kind of Court of Ladies, and you a page
Or favorite, a dwarf in jeans like theirs,
One of the group, all business, though inwardly
Half-drunk on glamour.
                              "Looking on the lines
Of my boy's face," the girl who plays your father
Pronounces, in lines you say from memory
As I drive you to rehearsal, "I did recoil
Twenty-three years, and saw myself unbreeched,
In my green velvet coat; my dagger muzzled,
Lest it should bite its master, and so prove,
As ornaments oft do, too dangerous."

Children are dangerous hostages to fortune—
Though they may seem, as to that fallible king,
Ornaments to our sentimental past,
They bind us to the future: Hope and Fear;
And though we might recoil, they make us strain
To see the wintry desert out beyond us.

On Opening Night, in hose and velvet tunic,
You say, *"a sad tale's best for winter"*—and yet,
The ending is happy; though the Bear eats the man,
Though the pastoral is broken, and the King alone
Upon the wind-scarred peak of his regret,
It all comes right: the statue comes to life,
And frozen Possibility moves and breathes,
Refreshed again, although the King is older.
Though happy endings rarely satisfy,
That one's a model of successful failure,
Holding Truth up against the rules of Romance.

The repetitious Phoenix, on her nest
Of burning contradictions, affronts belief
Like some impossible happy ending, as though
The country were just a dream—a pastoral
Delusion of the dirt and rocks and trees,
Or daydream of Leviathan himself,
A Romance of implausible rebirths.

The mountains intimate a different kind
Of ending: a cold and motionless remove.
High up above the treeline the clear dry air
Even in the warmest August noon conveys
A hint of snow; a crystal needle tickles
The nostrils a little, even while the eyes
Water and squint against the gray rock flashing,

The brightness of the sky.
                              In the Sierras,
Where Winter's never far, the country is clear,
A stage of granite swept for meditation—
Irrelevant to the saunas, Volkswagens and woks
As British mountains are to tea and curry,
The exotic and assimilated clutter
Of treasure that expansion washed ashore.
Up there, a miner or drifter might expand
Upon his solitude and drift away
Over the ridges deep in muffling snow,
Feel free from all the clutter of hopes and fears,
And let his breath diffuse in the lucid cold.

Nothing can seem more final than the mountains,
Where Empires seem to grow and fade like moss—
But even mountains have come to need protection,
By special laws and organized committees,
From our ingenuities, optimism, needs.
The passion to make new beginnings can shatter
The highest solitude, or living rock. . . .

One might end with disgust for such renewals:
The old bear lumbers from the hibernation
Of all his crimes and losses; the new sunlight,
Resurgent, falls in a halo on his grizzle,
And he feels young again—*America,*
The air that serves me with the breath to speak . . .
In the "Minnesota Belt" from Times Square west

For five blocks, children, boy and girl blonde hustlers
Imported from the Midwest, haunt all night—
Just as young children were sold in the Haymarket
Of William Morris's London, or the bazaars
Of ancient, drowsy Empires. But "It avails not,
Time nor place, distance avails not"; the country shrugs,
It is a cruel young profile from a coin,
Innocent and immortal in the religion
Of its own founding, and whatever happens
In actual New York, it is not final,
But a mere episode . . . and on some stage
As bare and rarefied as the coldest mountain,
With an authority transcending power
Or even belief, New Hope is born again,
And though it demand an Aztec vivisection
Everything lost must be made whole again.

A sad tale's best for winter, but the country
Sprawls over several zones of time and climate,
Never with any one season: the year itself
In no fixed place. Where nothing will stand still
Nothing can end—but recoils into the past,
Or is improvised into the dream or nightmare
Romance of new beginnings.
                              On a lake
Beyond the fastness of a mountain pass
The Asian settlers built a dazzling city
Of terraced fountains and mosaic walls,
With rainbow-colored carp and garish birds

To adorn the public gardens. In the streets,
The artisans of feathers, bark or silk
Traded with trappers, with French and Spanish priests
And Scottish grocers. From the distant peaks,
The fabulous creatures of the past descended
To barter or to take wives: minotaur
And centaur clattered on the cobbled streets
With Norseman and Gipsy; from the ocean floor
The mermaid courtesans came to Baltimore,
New Orleans, Galveston, their gilded aquaria
Tended by powdered Blacks. Nothing was lost—
Or rather, nothing seemed to begin or end
In ways they could remember. The Founders made
A Union mystic yet rational, and sudden,
As if suckled by the very wolf of Rome . . .
Indentured paupers and criminals grew rich
Trading tobacco; molasses; cotton; and slaves
With names like horses, or from Scott or Plutarch.
In the mills, there was every kind of name,
With even "Yankee" a kind of *jankel* or Dutchman.
The Yankees pulled stones from the earth, to farm,
And when the glacial boulders were piled high,
Skilled masons came from Parma and Piacenza
And settled on Division Street and Oak Street
And on the narrow side streets between them. In winter,
Mr. Diehl hired Italian boys to help
Harvest the ice from Diehl's Pond onto sledges
And pack it into icehouses, where it kept
To be cut and delivered all summer long.

The Linden Apartments stand where Diehl's Pond was;
But even when I was little, the iceman came
To houses that had iceboxes, and we could beg
Splinters to suck, or maybe even a ride,
Sitting on wet floorboards and steaming tarps
As far as Saint Andrew's, or the V.F.W.
The Eagles, Elks, Moose, Masons each had a building:
I pictured them like illustrations from *Alice*.
As television came in, the lodges faded,
But people began to group together by hobbies,
Each hobby with its magazines and clubs;
My father still played baseball twice a week;
And even after you were born, the schools
And colleges were places set apart,
As of another time; and one time you
Performed in *The Winter's Tale*.
                                And at the end,
As people applauded louder and louder, you
Stood with young girls who wore gray wigs and beards,
All smiling and holding hands—as if the Tale
Had not been sad at all, or was all a dream,
And winter was elsewhere, howling on the mountains
Unthinkably old and huge and far away—
At the far opposite edge of our whole country,
So large, and strangely broken, and unforeseen.

MEMORIAL

(J.E. and N.M.S.)

Here lies a man. And here, a girl. They live
In the kind of artificial life we give

To birds or statues: imagining what they feel,
Or that like birds the dead each had one call,

Repeated, or a gesture that suspends
Their being in a forehead or the hands.

A man comes whistling from a house. The screen
Snaps shut behind him. Though there is no man

And no house, memory sends him to get tools
From a familiar shed, and so he strolls

Through summer shade to work on the family car.
He is my uncle, and fresh home from the war,

With little for me to remember him doing yet.
The clock of the cancer ticks in his body, or not,

Depending if it is there, or waits. The search
Of memory gains and fails like surf: the porch

And trim are painted cream, the shakes are stained.
The shadows could be painted (so little wind

Is blowing there) or stains on the crazy-paving
Of the front walk. . . . Or now, the shadows are moving:

Another house, unrelated; a woman says,
Is this your special boy, and the girl says, yes,

Moving her hand in mine. The clock in her, too—
As someone told me a month or two ago,

Months after it finally took her. A public building
Is where the house was: though a surf, unyielding

And sickly, seethes and eddies at the stones
Of the foundation. The dead are made of bronze,

But dying they were like birds with clocklike hearts—
Unthinkable, how much pain the tiny parts

Of even the smallest bird might yet contain.
We become larger than life in how much pain

Our bodies may encompass . . . all Titans in that,
Or heroic statues. Although there is no heat

Brimming in the fixed, memorial summer, the brows
Of lucid metal sweat a faint warm haze

As I try to think the pain I never saw.
Though there is no pain there, the small birds draw

Together in crowds above the houses—and cry
Over the surf: as if there were a day,

Memorial, marked on the calendar for dread
And pain and loss—although among the dead

Are no hurts, but only emblematic things;
No hospital beds, but a lifting of metal wings.